Christmas Comes Alive!

Christmas Comes Alive!

BY
Geneva M. Butz

ILLUSTRATED BY
Helen Siegl

Geneva M. Butz

The Pilgrim Press
NEW YORK

The scripture quotations have been adapted by the author from the *Revised
Standard Version of the Bible*, copyright 1946, 1955, and © 1971, 1973 by the
Division of Christian Education, National Council of Churches, and are used by
permission. The quotations at the beginning of "A Tradition Begins" and at the
end of "A Tradition Continues" are from Howard Thurman, *The Inward Journey*
(New York: Harper & Row, 1961), pp. 29 and 28. Copyright © 1961 by Howard
Thurman. Used by permission of Harper & Row, Publishers. The Meister Eckhart
quote in the Preface is from Matthew Fox, *Original Blessing* (Santa Fe:
Bear & Co., 1983), p. 106.

Library of Congress Cataloging-in-Publication Data

Butz, Geneva M., 1944–
　　Christmas comes alive!

　　1. Jesus Christ—Nativity—Meditations.　2. Crèches
(Nativity scenes)—Pennsylvania—Philadelphia.　I. Title.
BT315.2.B9　　1988　　232.9′2　　　88-19587
ISBN 0-8298-0787-X

The Pilgrim Press, 132 West 31 Street, New York, NY 10001

Contents

Preface   7

A Tradition Begins   9

1.   The Empty Stable   13
2.   They Don't All Stay   17
3.   The Whole World Comes   21
4.   Why Animals?   25
5.   What Is a Manger?   29
6.   Mary Falls Apart   33
7.   A Stand-in Joseph   37
8.   Everybody's Baby   41
9.   In the Shadow of Economic Power   47
10.   Is There Room in the Inn?   51
11.   Lost Sheep   55
12.   Death Comes to the Creche   61
13.   The Smelly Straw   65
14.   A Wise Man's Journey to the Manger   69
15.   The Fourth Wise Man   75
16.   A Meeting Place for Unity   79
17.   Go, Tell It!   83
18.   Lessons in Caring   87

A Tradition Continues   93

Preface

URING THE WEEKS preceding Christmas, I received both Christmas cards and sympathy cards. Just a month before the holiday, after only six weeks of illness, my dad died. What a jumble of emotions I felt. Christmas was approaching, but I was not really ready to go to the manger. The living Christmas creche was already in place at Old First Reformed Church, but its message seemed remote.

Then one Sunday morning one of the sheep in the creche died suddenly. I could hardly believe it! The message of the manger reached me where I hurt the most. Out of an encounter with the finality of death, something totally new was born in me.

What emerged were these real-life stories, which I had witnessed over the years as pastor of Old First Reformed Church. When death visited the Christmas creche, the stories that had been dormant inside of me came to life. The Christmas message of hope and new life touched me in a personal way. Meister Eckhart's words, from his Christmas Eve sermon of the fifteenth century, spoke to me: "What good is it to me if Mary gave birth to the Son of God 1,400 years ago and I don't give birth to God's Son in my person and my culture and my times?" At the manger, new life was waiting to be born.

Several people have supported me in the work of this book. I want to express my thanks to Marion M. Meyer of The Pilgrim Press for her encouragement and editorial work, to Rosemary Polo for typing the manuscript with cheer and goodwill, to the Rev. H. Daehler Hayes for creating the original Christmas creche at Fourth and Race, to Anthony Bonaccurso for, year after year, lending his animals for the holiday season, and to all the members of Old First Reformed Church, United Church of Christ, for their participation in the annual creche and their interest and delight in these stories.

A Tradition Begins

*In the center of a great modern city, a rustic creche
is placed, symbolizing an eternal message which must
ever anew find a temporal setting. The Christmas
gospel must be related to the needs of this world.*

*Christmas says: "Life keeps coming on, keeps
seeking to fulfill itself, keeps affirming the possibility
of hope."*

*Christmas means "one more thing to try when all
else has failed, the upward reach of life. It is the
incentive to carry on."*

THESE WORDS are printed on the plaque at the entrance to the living
Christmas creche at Old First Reformed Church, United Church of Christ.
This innovative creche has become a Christmas tradition in Center City
Philadelphia.

Each year, a few weeks before Christmas, members of the church put up
the large stable that houses a display of the nativity scene, featuring life-size
mannequins and live animals. People come from far and wide to see this
simple setting of the Christmas story. Some come upon the scene by accident
and cannot believe their eyes. Others make an annual pilgrimage, bringing
their friends and loved ones and even their out-of-town guests. On Christmas
Eve the mannequins are removed and real people, members of Old First,
dramatize the Christmas story in tableau form.

The living Christmas creche is located in a very historic place. Not only is it three blocks from Independence Hall and the Liberty Bell, but it is also on the exact spot where Philadelphia's first German Reformed Church stood, a small, six-sided structure built in 1747 by the Rev. Michael Schlatter. That same year the building was the site of the first Coetus (synod) of the struggling German Reformed congregations from nearby New Jersey, Maryland, and the surrounding Pennsylvania countryside. At that gathering, under Schlatter's leadership, the German Reformed Church began as a denomination in the United States.

But times changed. In 1774 the quaint, German-looking church gave way to a larger colonial Georgian building. An enlargement of that building, completed in 1837, now houses the current congregation.

The neighborhood has seen changes as well. Once a residential area for the German-speaking population of Philadelphia, it was on the outskirts of colonial Philadelphia. In the nineteenth century, with the advent of the industrial revolution, people moved from the area to the expanding northern part of the city. The church also relocated, selling its building to the Lucas Paint Company. Factories and warehouses took over the Delaware River waterfront area. In recent years these factories and warehouses have been converted to condominiums and apartments. People have been moving back to the historic Old City. Old First returned, in 1967, to restore its former building and to reclaim its history in the place where it first began.

The live-animal Christmas creche emerged in 1973 out of the rubble of the restoration project. Small buildings attached to the historic church by the Lucas Paint Company were demolished. The Rev. H. Daehler Hayes, pastor of Old First at the time, found enough large timbers in the debris to construct a simple shed. Then he contacted a friend who raised livestock and was willing to bring in animals for the two-week holiday period. The tradition of the living Christmas creche at Fourth and Race Streets was launched.

But the custom of the Christmas creche goes back to the year 1223, when Francis of Assisi set up the first creche at the grotto of Greccio in Italy. He wanted to make the humanity of Jesus more real to the people of his day. The first manger was even used as an altar, as Francis invited people of the area surrounding Greccio to a solemn mass, celebrated over the crib. Francis, a deacon, preached at the event. According to tradition, an infant appeared to come to life in the crib as Francis spoke. The idea of the creche caught on. Today there are Christmas creches in all parts of the world.

Old First's living Christmas creche at Fourth and Race is in marked contrast to the bright lights and hectic pace of noisy downtown Philadelphia. People rush by on their way to work or on their way home from shopping. The commercial agenda is everywhere—from the U.S. Mint across the street to nearby restaurants, factories, offices, and shops. And yet, somehow the simple scene speaks. The setting disarms people as they encounter the Christmas story in the midst of routine life.

The living Christmas creche has all the appeal and all the risk of real life. The congregation and the neighbors enjoy the unpredictable events that occur around the manger. The one most people remember took place the year there was a camel. Standing eight feet tall and weighing more than 2,000 pounds, the camel insisted on eating the costumes off the mannequins. Mr. Hayes had to rush to the creche to drape the nude nativity figures with blankets.

Knowledge of Jesus' birth is rather uncertain. The biblical accounts do not even agree. No eyewitness reporters were at the holy birth. But how the story really happened is not as important as how the message touches us today. The living Christmas creche is Old First's proclamation of the good news of its faith to all the people of Philadelphia. The church does it boldly by taking the story from the pages of the Bible and setting it up on the street corner where people can easily see it, feel it, and relate to it. The story is given life, the power of the message "God with us" is felt, and the good news lives as it touches people's lives.

I

The Empty Stable

THE STABLE IS the centerpiece of our live-animal Christmas creche. Usually the Saturday after Thanksgiving is when Earl, the two Johns, Barry, Buzzy, Julio, and others gather to construct it. We use the same sides and fence and roof each year, so the men carry the big pieces outside, reassemble them, and patch or rebuild the pieces that have deteriorated over the past year.

The major work can be completed in a day, at least with a full team of eight to ten workers. Barry, Buzzy, and Julio are expert carpenters; they know exactly what to do. My job, coaching from the sidelines, is to encourage the men to slap it together, not caring whether the corners are exactly even or whether everything is perfectly matched. "This is a crude stable, a shack, a lean-to, and shouldn't look too secure," I argue. It's a challenge to the workers' professionalism to build a structure that appears obviously shoddy.

At the end of the big workday the major pieces have been put in place. John, Earl, and Bill add the finishing touches during the following weeks. There are spotlights to be set on an electric timer, plaques with biblical readings from the Christmas story to be nailed to the fence, tar paper to be tacked to the roof, straw to be spread on the floor. To avoid the possibility of having to work in uncooperative weather, all is readied days in advance. Then the stable sits there—empty, waiting for the animals to arrive.

"When will the animals get here?" six-year-old Kevin anxiously asks his grandmother as they round the corner into the church courtyard. It's the second Sunday in Advent, and the stable is still empty. For two Sundays in a row Kevin has come to church expecting to see the creche with the animals inside, and still there is no sign of life. For a little boy, the wait seems endless; for us adults, the emptiness questions our fully scheduled and immediately satisfied lives.

How long will it take? How stripped must we become? How do we prepare to receive the Messiah in a world that sees Christmas as a commercial holiday, a time for parties and shopping and gift-giving? Can Christ be born into our logical and overly structured world?

The creche sits there empty, challenging our agendas and our priorities, our goodwill, and even our somewhat stilted faith. Will God touch us once again with a gift so full of wonder and awe? Can we discover the child within us, with its tender trust and ever-joyful hope? Are we open to be delighted by the surprising ways in which God chooses to visit us?

Israel's longing for a Messiah was kept alive over centuries. Will our Advent-wait enable God's holiness to enliven us?

2

They Don't All Stay

IT IS 8:45 AM when the driver pulls up to the corner of Fourth and Race Streets with a trailer filled with animals for our Christmas creche. The trailer has arrived right in the middle of rush-hour traffic. Our corner is one of the busiest intersections in Philadelphia. Cars and trucks converge on Fourth Street, just two blocks from the only Center City off-ramp for Interstate 95, a major artery that carries hundreds of commuters to work in downtown Philadelphia each morning.

The trailer stops on Fourth Street, blocking one lane of traffic. Cars have to merge to the right-hand lane. Philadelphia streets are narrow, especially in Old City and nearby Independence Mall. Usually drivers shake their fists, blow their horns, or get out of their cars and start yelling impatiently at any obstruction that blocks their way, particularly at this hour of the morning. But today most drivers seem to slow down in order to get a better look. What's this, animals in the city? On the way to work, no one expects to see sheep and donkeys and a cow!

Earl has come to help place the mannequins and wait with me for the animals to arrive. We also have to put out feed and fill the water troughs. Then our job is to open and close the gate as, one by one, the animals are led into the fenced-in area around the creche. We are to make sure that once inside the fence, none of the animals can escape.

First the sheep go in. They are quite cooperative. After all, they can be picked up and carried into the creche in the farmer's arms, if they don't walk in on their four legs. The donkeys wear halters. They come out next and are easy to manage. Last comes the cow. One person leads the cow by a rope tied to her neck. A second person holds her from the rear by her tail.

Now, what's wrong with the cow? She doesn't seem to want to come out of the trailer. This cow is very stubborn. The farmhands give her a shove, and she steps out onto the pavement. So they just need to lead her in through the fence. Earl and I have the gate open. But the cow decides to go in another direction. She rears up on her hind legs and runs off into the churchyard. The farmhands are still holding onto the rope and her tail. Now they both grab the rope, trying to pin her down, but she drags them, and finally, not to get hurt, they let go. Off she goes into the street! Cars screech to a halt. The farmhands are in pursuit. Earl and I can hardly bear to watch.

It has been raining. When her hoofs hit the wet asphalt, the cow skids and falls, right in the middle of the intersection. She gets up and runs into the Pincus Brothers parking lot across the street. This area has a big brick wall around it, so we breathe a sigh of relief. The farmhands have made it into the parking lot. Meanwhile all traffic is at a standstill, and the occupants of the cars are laughing at the comic scene that is unfolding before their eyes. Wait until they get to the office and tell their co-workers what happened on the way downtown! No one will believe this!

A telephone repairworker appears out of nowhere with a good strong rope, and the cow is securely fastened to a post in the clothing factory parking lot. Pincus employees have left their machines, and everywhere people are peering out of doors and windows. Live animals make our creche very unpredictable. The cow has made her debut in the city, but unfortunately she cannot stay. She is too unruly. This year our creche will be minus a cow. It is better to have one less animal than to risk turmoil in the manger.

3

The Whole World Comes

From THE VERY BEGINNING, just minutes after the animals arrive, people start coming to view the creche. It seems as if the animals act as a magnet, pulling visitors in off the street. No one expects to see animals at Fourth and Race. People are at once disarmed and charmed.

Sometimes a whole class of preschoolers walks to the stable, accompanied by teachers. Parents bring their youngsters, some of them still infants wrapped in blankets and carried in their parents' arms. Older children like to feed the animals and come loaded down with bags of carrots and apples.

The homeless who wander the streets of Center City daily seek out the creche. They're among those I've observed regularly relating to the scene. Sometimes they carry on long conversations with the donkeys or the cow.

Teenagers out on the town, looking for ways to spend their money and their time, come by. One afternoon I noticed a whole group of young people playing with the animals. I went over to chat with the teenagers and learned that they were residents of a drug rehabilitation facility, enjoying some free time in Center City.

Foreign visitors of all nations and races and faiths are brought by their American hosts. Some hear the Christmas story for the first time at our creche.

The elderly come, accompanied by their families and assisted by canes and walkers. They hobble across busy Fourth Street. Sometimes I fear for their safety, as the traffic going by has far more speed than they do.

Buses slow down, taxis stop, and even the Philadelphia police are moved to come for a closer look. One morning an off-duty police officer parked across the street and got out of his car. "I was wondering what this was," he said to Janet and Connie, who were giving the animals their early-morning breakfast. "Last night my partner and I stopped across the street, waiting for the traffic light to change. I thought I saw something move over here, but my partner said, 'Get out, you've been up too long!' Now I know I saw something move. What's this all about, anyway?"

There are TV newscasters with their camera crews, women in fur coats on their way to Christmas parties, neighbors walking their dogs. One day Debbie ran into the church office to report, "Hey, there are nuns out there, and they're praying!"

The whole world comes to the creche. Everybody is attracted by the simple story. The creche pulls people of all faiths—and even those with no faith—in for a closer look.

4

Why Animals?

A Muslim friend from Iran was standing at the creche one day. "Hossein," I coaxed, "we need you in our pageant on Christmas Eve. It was people from your country who were the wise men from the East, who followed the star to the stable and found Jesus and his parents there. We usually have someone from the Middle East in the pageant, but this year he can't make it. Wouldn't you like to dress up as one of the wise men? You'd look great in the costume!"

"Oh, yes, the wise men were from Persia, as my country was formerly called," he said proudly. "But I don't like animals. I'm afraid to go into the stable. That cow has horns! I prefer to stay on this side of the fence."

Later, as we were drinking coffee in the parsonage, Hossein began thinking more about the creche. "There's something I don't understand," he pondered. "May I ask you a question? Why animals? What is the meaning of the animals?"

I hadn't thought about it really. I had always taken it for granted that Jesus was born in a stable and that the animals were there. They, along with Mary and Joseph, were the first witnesses to the incarnation. But when Hossein asked the question, I began to think about the animals. How profound! Jesus was born in the midst of the animal world. Did the unique circumstances of his birth give a new respect to the animals? Did Jesus' coming in this specific way restore harmony between the human and animal worlds? Did Jesus' birth give a new integrity to the created order? Thanks to the question of my non-Christian friend, I discovered that Jesus' coming brought reconciliation on a much grander scale than I had ever before considered!

5

What Is a Manger?

WHAT IS A MANGER? Ask any of the children at Old First Church and they will tell you. It is the place where the animals get their hay. Even though the children may not know that the word manger is the same as the common French word *manger* (mā' zhe), meaning "to eat," they have often watched the animals feed at the large manger near the fence of the living Christmas creche.

The children know our creche has another manger, a much smaller, lower one at the center of the stable. Here's where the baby Jesus "laid down his sweet head," as it says in the song they like to sing. This is the focal point of every Christmas creche. It's where God placed the real food—satisfying bread, the bread of life.

When believers come to the manger, they come to be fed by this life-giving food, the living Christ. The manger is the altar upon which the bread of life is given. Here is where nourishing food is broken open for us.

The animals seem to have a eucharistic instinct too. They know where the best food is. Instead of eating only from the large manger, where hay awaits them in abundance, they like to nibble the hay from the low manger, where Jesus lies. Even our putting ropes or boards in front of the small manger does not stop the animals from going to this source for life-giving food.

A manger is a good place to look if you are hungry. Some find only hay; others, the bread of life.

6

Mary Falls Apart

Y ES, MARY FALLS APART. It happens frequently. When a group of us returned to the church after Christmas caroling in the Old City neighborhood, Mary had fallen apart again. Even though John ropes off the part of the creche where the mannequins are, the sheep get in there. They like to snuggle close to Mary and nestle in the folds of her robe. When they stand up and turn around . . . oops, they push Mary off her seat. She tumbles into the hay. At other times the wind whips through the creche and catches Mary's hair, and she falls again. It looks so funny to see Mary, usually the model of serenity and composure, lying on the ground, sometimes in awkward, even comical, positions.

When I see Mary lying on the ground like that, I find her so very human. It seems fitting that she should be dismayed, overwhelmed, shattered, even broken by the events that have just happened to her. What one of us would not be devastated by the happenings surrounding the birth of Jesus? The angel comes to her and tells her that she is to bear a child whose name will be called Jesus, who will be a child of the Most High God. Mary must have worried about this news. How will she face Joseph, to whom she is engaged? How will her parents react? What will the neighbors say? When a child is born to an unwed mother, it is a devastating experience, even in our day. Mary's words, "How can this be, since I have no husband?" have been soul-searchingly repeated by many women around the world who find themselves in a similarly awkward position. If Mary is human, then Mary most certainly does what all the rest of us do when faced with such alarming news—Mary falls apart.

The amazing part of the story is that eventually Mary chooses to believe what the angel told her. I'm sure it didn't happen all at once. It took time for Mary to get it all together. She must have questioned and struggled with the news. But finally Mary chooses to believe all that the angel had proclaimed to her, "With God nothing is impossible." Then Mary can affirm, "Let it be done to me according to your word."

Mary makes a journey of trust, from disbelief and dismay to acceptance and even affirmation of all that the angel has said. Mary believes that God's hand is upon her in a special way and that the child to be born to her will be holy.

Ultimately, Mary is able to trust God. She is able to face the way things are in her life, rather than the way she would like them to be. She is able to acknowledge that life is not turning out the way she wants it to be. Mary is able to accept the unacceptable, the unresolved nature of things. And so must we! To really trust is to refrain from having to know all the answers ahead of time, or having to control all that will happen to us. To trust means to be able to leave some empty spaces when we fall apart. To trust is to let go and leave room so that God can indeed work a new thing in and through us.

When I used this story as an illustration in a sermon the Sunday before Christmas, the church secretary inadvertently typed "Many Fall Apart" as the sermon title in the Sunday bulletin. Her title fits, too, for *many* of us *do* fall apart. I was amazed at the number of parishioners who identified with Mary and could tell me so at the door that Sunday morning. Suddenly they had words to describe, and felt it all right to admit, that, like Mary, they, too, sometimes fall apart.

7

A Stand-in Joseph

On Christmas Eve the mannequins are removed from the creche, and Old First members play the parts of the holy family, the shepherds, and the wise men. Usually we have a baby, born a few weeks before, who is strong enough to be placed in the manger even in the coldest weather. The baby determines what parents will play the roles of Mary and Joseph. (How like the biblical story!) But sometimes we have a baby with only the mother present—and then we have to look for a stand-in Joseph.

It happened one year. Mary and the baby arrived on time, but Joseph had to work. So, while the shepherds, wise men, and Mary were dressing, I went out to the crowd that had assembled to view the pageant and picked out a bearded man, a complete stranger whom I thought "looked the part."

"How would you like to be Joseph tonight?" I asked him. "Mary and the baby are here, but Joseph couldn't make it. Would you play his role?"

The stranger readily agreed, went inside, put on Joseph's robe, and took his place next to Mary and the baby. No one would have guessed that Joseph wasn't the real father.

Was it like that with Jesus' father too? Could anyone have guessed that Joseph wasn't the real father of Jesus? Did he look the part?

When the pageant was over, the stranger took off Joseph's robe, and, before we had a chance to learn his real name, he disappeared. We didn't even thank him for playing the part.

The biblical Joseph seems to disappear after the birth narrative too. We hear little of him again. Mary, Jesus' mother, is at the wedding at Cana at the beginning of Jesus' ministry, and she is also at the foot of the cross on the day of Jesus' death. But where is Joseph? We don't learn any more about him. He never appears during Jesus' public ministry. Some scholars believe that Joseph died an early death, leaving Mary a widow.

In Matthew's Gospel, however, Joseph plays a main role in the birth story. It is Joseph, rather than Mary, who is the central figure. This Joseph, like the Old Testament ancestor whose name he bears, has a special sensitivity to dreams and the interior life. An angel appears to him in one of his dreams and tells him to go ahead and marry Mary, even though she is pregnant, for the child she awaits was conceived by the Holy Spirit. Joseph is to name the child, thereby taking legal responsibility for the baby in the eyes of society.

Because Joseph obeys and does what the angel tells him to do, Jesus is linked to the house of David and is an offspring of the root of Jesse. He is given, not just a legal name, but a specific heritage among a people with whom God has a special relationship.

Later, when the baby's life is in danger, Joseph again responds to a dream and takes Mary and the babe to Egypt, where they will be safe from Herod's slaughter of the Hebrew children. Thus Jesus, "the one who saves," is saved for the salvation of the world. Jesus continues the long line of history and liberation begun in the Old Testament, thanks to Joseph, his stand-in father, who is just as important to the Christmas story as is Mary.

8

Everybody's Baby

EVERY YEAR, GOD GIVES us a real live baby, born to one of our church families during the weeks before Christmas, to play the role of Jesus in the live nativity tableau presented on Christmas Eve. One of our members recently commented on the babies who have played the role of Jesus: "Sometimes the baby is black; sometimes the baby is white; sometimes the baby is the first-born; sometimes the baby is the second-born; sometimes the baby is a boy; sometimes the baby is a girl. What a wonderful reminder that God came to humankind in the form of a baby and continues to come to us in unexpected people!" Yes, many children at Old First have had the opportunity to be placed in the manger and to take the part of Jesus.

Last Christmas Eve, Rae brought her three-year-old son Steven, for a closer look at the baby Jesus. Steven had a wonderful smile on his face as they came near to where Yolanda was sitting with this year's baby, Jonathan. As Steven was getting his first good look at the baby, Rae told him, "Steven, three years ago *you* were the baby Jesus!" His eyes widened and his face brightened as he began to comprehend his mother's words. What a wonderful experience for Steven (baptized with water and the Holy Spirit, claimed by God, and carrying the name of Christ) to know that he, too, had once lain in the manger where Jesus was laid.

Once the baby is placed in the manger, the baby becomes the universal child. The infant is there for everybody. The holy child becomes everybody's baby.

In order really to understand this, we have to leave the manger and go to the temple. Forty days after Jesus' birth, according to Luke's Gospel, Mary and Joseph took the baby to the temple in Jerusalem to be presented to God, as was the custom in those days. According to Jewish law, the first-born son had to be taken to the temple, sacrifices offered, and the child dedicated to God. There, in the temple, were two aged people, Anna and Simeon. Both of them were reported to be more than one hundred years old. They had been closely associated with the temple over the years. Now both of them spent most of their days and nights fasting and praying there, awaiting the future hope of Israel.

When Mary and Joseph brought the baby to the temple, Anna and Simeon came to see him. They reached out to touch him and hold him in their arms. They recognized Jesus as being *their* baby as well. For them, this infant was the hope they had been waiting for all these years. They saw in him, not just the salvation of Israel, but a light for the gentiles. Here was the universal baby, around whom all the nations of the world would gather.

Perhaps the elderly—people who have been faithful over the years—are more likely to have the vision to recognize just who Jesus really is. When they touched him, Anna and Simeon were connected with the future hope of all people. What a joy, what a blessing for them! Anna and Simeon thanked God for this child, and blessed Jesus. Their lives were complete; their hopes had been satisfied; their waiting was fulfilled. Simeon was able to sing: "Now let your servant depart in peace, according to your word, for my eyes have seen your salvation."

To see how the baby who plays the part of Jesus in the creche is everybody's baby, we, too, need to take him out of the manger and present her in the church, to be dedicated to God and given to the faith community. When the baby is brought into the church, many other people who have been faithful over the years will be there to welcome her as their baby, to receive him into their own family.

At Old First we have many members who are eighty years of age and older. Most of them are very active, generous in their giving to the church, and regularly present for worship each week. What hope a new baby, brought into the church, is for them! Hope for people like Owen, for example, our 87-year-old patriarch, whose main work in life was leading the congregation back to its original building at Fourth and Race Streets and restoring the paint factory to its former use as a church; hope for Ruth, 92, who is at the front door every Sunday morning, greeting all who come! Both of these aged people have lived the most significant part of their lives in the church. The church is where meaning and hope continue to be realized for them. What a joy as each new baby comes, for each child is, in some mysterious way, born to Ruth and Owen as well. Each child means a future for the church they love so much.

9

*In the Shadow
of Economic Power*

Ba-boom, ba-boom, ba-boom, ba-boom. The ground beneath the creche reverberates with a steady beat. No, it's not a nearby disco, nor someone's stereo with the volume blasting. It's the vibration of the presses at the U.S. Mint across the street, pounding out nickels, dimes, quarters, and pennies, pennies, pennies. It's the heartbeat of capitalism, compulsively producing more, more, more. It's the money factory at work, pounding out coins that are valued at more than one million dollars a day.

The cow chews her cud; the donkeys bask in the sun; Mary sits serenely watching the babe. They seem to be unaware of the steady beat. Ba-boom, ba-boom, ba-boom, the beat goes on. Pennies, as many as thirty-five million a day, bounce off the presses and glitter as they slide along the computerized conveyor belts. "In God We Trust," "In God We Trust," "In God We Trust," the coins proclaim.

The huge, pink granite building, housing one of only two mints in the United States, dominates the neighborhood. Set on a five-acre plot, the building occupies one complete city block. Tourists, as many as a quarter of a million a year, stream in to see money being made. The tiny creche is barely noticeable as it sits in the shadow of the mint's gigantic structure. The solid granite walls and sophisticated security system of the mint are a striking contrast to the clapboard sides of the creche as they stand unprotected on a small 10′ × 14′ patch of ground. God's power seems so vulnerable, so defenseless, so meek in the face of the economic reality of our day. "Money talks, " we like to say. "Money buys power," we acknowledge. But God's power cannot be bought or sold. And ultimately money does not satisfy the needs of the human heart. The marketplace mentality cannot prevail. "Make justice your aim," the prophets cry.

Jesus was born in the midst of political and economic oppression. Mary and Joseph went to Bethlehem to be counted in the census decreed by the Roman Emperor Caesar Augustus. Quirinius was governor of Syria. All went to be enrolled and to be taxed. But Mary's song proclaimed God's justice:

> *God has scattered the proud in the imagination of their hearts,*
> *God has put down the mighty from their thrones,*
> *and exalted those of low degree;*
> *God has filled the hungry with good things,*
> *and the rich sent empty away.*
> *God has helped God's servant Israel,*
> *in remembrance of God's mercy.*
> —Luke 1:51–54

This infant, born into a troubled world, turned over the tables of the money changers, preached good news to the poor, and announced God's reign. Jesus showed us a way of life in which we could live as brothers and sisters, showing mercy and living compassionately. That possibility begins at the manger, where God's power takes on the vulnerability of human flesh.

10

Is There Room in the Inn?

O
N MANY A NIGHT in Philadelphia there are hundreds of people sleeping in abandoned buildings, in back alleys, or down under, in the subway concourse. Yes, there are even people who sleep on the street corners, on the steam vents, right in full view of all who pass by. The homeless population in Philadelphia numbers in the thousands. There is not nearly enough afford-able housing for everyone. There is no room for the poor. Homelessness in America reaches into every community, suburban and rural, as well as into our urban centers. It is a crisis, but most of us prefer not to see it.

Perhaps the people in our society who understand the Christmas story best are the homeless. They know what it's like to go begging for food and for a place to come in out of the cold. They, too, look for room in the inn and are told that the inn is full. So they have to go out and find a makeshift place to sleep, sometimes moving each evening. The homeless are not all alcoholic drifters. There are men and women and children—whole families—who have been forced into this way of life.

A few years ago two Sisters of Mercy went to all the churches in Center City Philadelphia, asking the congregations if they would open their doors to the homeless during the winter months. The Sisters had been running a hospice for women for the past six years, and now they were looking for space to house men. They also foresaw an increase in the homeless popula-tion because of recent changes in the welfare laws.

After the Sisters came to Old First, their request was taken to the Official Board of the church. At first there was some skepticism. Where would the men shower? How would we feed them? Who would supervise the project and be able to stay awake all night? How would we meet medical and more long-term needs? But even before solutions to all these concerns were found, the Board voted to go ahead and to allow twenty homeless men into the church social hall each evening. Perhaps the story of the Christmas creche had opened our hearts so that we could risk making room for those who hurt in our day.

The homeless have been a blessing to us at Old First over the years. We have already had an emergency shelter for five years during the winter months. The men who stay there each night have helped us to realize the deeper meaning of the Christmas story, as we are challenged to share more and more of what is ours with those who need.

I meet weekly with the men of the shelter for a time of prayer. When the Christmas creche is built and the animals arrive, of course the men become interested. One night I asked them what they noticed about the scene. One of them said, "I've been observing the sheep. They're so timid. They're always hiding in the back. The cow is big and out front and can get to the food first. The donkeys are real cute and get all the attention. But who's taking care of the sheep? They really need strengthening."

The Gospel of John says that Jesus asked Peter three times, "Do you love me?" Each time Peter responded, "Lord, you know that I do." Jesus said, "Then, feed my sheep."

II

Lost Sheep

I RETURNED FROM A TRIP to Princeton, less than a two-hour drive north of Philadelphia. The animals had arrived that morning, but I had thought it safe to make a trip out of town for a few hours.

It was almost dusk when I pulled into the church driveway and headed for my office. Ed met me at the creche and excitedly reported the news. "The sheep are missing. They've been gone about an hour. We've looked everywhere for them. See, there's a hole in the back of the stable." He rushed me to the rear of the creche, and sure enough, there was a hole just wide enough for sheep to squeeze through.

"Lois has been out looking in all the back alleys of Old City," Ed continued. Just then Lois arrived. "No sheep anywhere," she sighed. Together we searched behind the church building one more time, thinking they just *had* to be hiding there.

What to do now? I'm sure the sheep aren't covered by our insurance policy, I thought. How could this have happened? Did someone steal the sheep, or did they run away of their own accord? How will I face the farmer? What kind of a pastor am I anyway, to let my sheep get loose? How will I ever find them?

I recalled my first Christmas Eve at Old First. As the shepherds entered the tableau, I announced their arrival with the familiar words from Luke's Gospel. Suddenly a sheep appeared at the front of the stable! One at a time, the other two sheep came out to the people. All three had heard my voice and responded, right on time!

But now three sheep were missing. They had wandered off while I was out of town. Well, what does an urban pastor do when she loses her sheep? Yes, I did; I phoned the police!

"Sure, Lady," the voice on the other end of the telephone replied. "You lost your sheep. And I guess your name is Bo Peep too. Right?"

"No," I pleaded. "I really did lose three sheep. I'm the pastor of the church at Fourth and Race Streets, which has the live-animal Christmas creche. The animals arrived this morning, and now three sheep are missing. There's a big hole in the back of the stable too."

"OK, we'll send a car right away!" the officer said, as he hung up.

A police car appeared in a few minutes. The officer was courteous and listened patiently to our story. We showed him the hole in the rear of the stable, and then he asked me to sit in the police car so I could help him write a report. He wanted a description of the animals. "Funny," he muttered, "that no one called in. You'd think anyone seeing sheep wandering freely through the city would call the cops. I'll check again to see if anyone's made a report."

No one had reported seeing our missing sheep. "OK," he said, "I'll put it on the radio, and we'll get an all-points bulletin out right away. Meanwhile I'll drive through the back streets of Old City to see if I can find them. I'll be in touch."

I went back to the creche again. "Where are my sheep?" I cried. There was nothing to do but to go inside the church office and wait. I thought I should telephone the church trustees to let them know what had happened. Also, I'd better get our carpenters back to repair the hole. Before I realize it, the donkeys, and maybe even the cow, will break out!

I was sitting at my desk, talking to one of the trustees, when all of a sudden the lights went on in the creche. Night had fallen, and the automatic timer had triggered the lights. Out frolicked the three sheep, quite inno-

---

cently. I could barely believe my eyes. They were back! The sheep had returned.

I ran out to the creche, crying, "The sheep are found! The lost sheep have come home!" There was no one there to hear me, but I just had to shout it!

Well, guess what? The sheep had never wandered away. They had been in the back of the stable all along, lying down among the folds of Mary's robe. They must have battered the hole in the stable wall, but they had never run away. It had been dusk, and no one had seen them, hiding there in the straw.

Could this be the case with church members who we think have left the institutional church, I wondered. The back door may be open, but many of our "lost" members haven't gone out. Can we see them? Are we looking in the right place? They are still hiding in the membership rolls. And especially at Christmas, they nestle very close to Mary.

12

Death Comes to the Creche

N̲o one expects to find death in the Christmas creche. But that's what was happening.

As I rounded the corner from the parsonage to the Parish House one Sunday morning, Janet called me. "There's something wrong with the sheep. It seems real sick." By this time Janet was kneeling beside the lamb. It was lying right out front at the fence. This was very un-sheeplike behavior, I thought. The other sheep were still in the back of the stable. The cow and the donkeys were right up front and were nudging the little sheep. Janet tried to keep them away. She reported that the sheep's breathing was very slow. "I think it's dying. What do we do now?"

What *do* we do now? None of the animals at our creche had ever died before. I didn't know what to do. I decided to telephone the farmer in New Jersey who so graciously lends us the animals each year.

The farmer took my news quite calmly. I suppose he's more used to sheep dying than I am. "We saw no sign of foul play, and the other animals seem to be OK," I added, trying to be cheerful. Actually the sheep are the least vulnerable of all the animals because they stay to the back of the stable. They're not prone to take food from strangers or eat anything but the hay and corn mixture we put out.

"I'll be over at noon," the farmer replied. That's almost three hours from now, I thought. What will we do in the meantime?

People were already gathering for Sunday morning worship. "A lamb is dying," I whispered. "Yes, a lamb is dying, out in the Christmas creche. Who will stand there and help people deal with it?" This was not the easiest job to ask people to do, but somebody had to help those coming to find life, prepare for death. One of our deacons volunteered, but when she got to the creche, she found Janet there. Janet had returned to the dying lamb; she would help visitors understand what was happening.

The farmer arrived just before noon, while the congregation (except Janet) was still inside worshiping. I never did see him. I was probably giving my sermon, ironically titled "Disarming Ourselves." Meanwhile, outside at the creche, death, the ultimate enemy, the final disarmer, was having its say! The farmer took the dead lamb home to New Jersey.

No one expects to find death in the Christmas creche. But if we do not find it there, if we see only Jesus' birth, we have missed the deeper purpose behind his coming. Christ is God's lamb, God's gift of perfect love. God's lamb died that we might know life even more fully.

13

The Smelly Straw

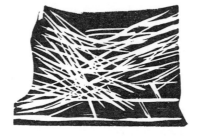

WHEN THE ANIMALS first arrive and we have put out fresh straw, the creche looks beautiful—so warm and inviting. Who wouldn't want to sleep there?

But after the animals have lived in the stable for a week or so, the straw becomes messy. The stable becomes real and takes on an authentic odor. You cannot have a living creche without the stench of the animals.

By the time Christmas Eve approaches, one really has a sense that the world into which Jesus comes is quite smelly. It isn't a quaint, cozy stall, but a smelly stable into which Christ is born.

Just before New Year's Eve the animals leave. After the holiday we dismantle the creche, and all the pieces of the stable go back into storage. What remains are the memories of the great visitation, the joy so many people have had—and the messy, decaying straw.

There it sits for weeks on end. It snows. The muck freezes. We wait for a thaw, so that the maintenance crew from the Philadelphia Protestant Home (a retirement community) can come to get it.

Meanwhile it's there. We pass by it and are reminded of the dark side of the incarnation, the dark reality of the world in which we all live and into which Jesus was born. The leftover mess is the part of life we try to avoid. One of my ministerial colleagues remarked when he came to the church for a meeting, "Geneva, most of us don't put it right out by the front door!"

The dark, smelly, rotting, stinking side of life, and of ourselves, is what we try to cover over. Call it our fears, our angers, our doubts. All that is unexplainable is included in this darkness: pain, suffering, the death of a loved one, a sudden illness, loss of a relationship, an unwelcome change of job. Our world is wrapped in darkness, and we cannot, nor should not, run from it.

Jesus was able to embrace the dark side of the human condition. He humbled himself to become part of the earth, to become one of us, to enter this "humus." In doing so Jesus was able to embrace the darkness, even the darkness of the tomb, and to redeem it.

The dying process is a natural part of life. There is an inevitability in the decay of all things. Jesus helps us to face the darkness of the human condition without fear and see in it the potential for new growth.

By the time spring has come, all the smelly straw has been scattered on the gardens of senior citizens at the Philadelphia Protestant Home. The muck, which we are tempted to discard, can also be embraced. It can become fertilizer, helping produce delicious tomatoes and strawberries to please our palates, and beautiful flowers to delight our senses.

14

*A Wise Man's Journey
to the Manger*

I<small>T WAS</small> S<small>EPTEMBER</small>, the day after Labor Day, 1983. I received a phone call from a man who was a patient in Metropolitan Hospital, just four blocks from the church, at Eighth and Race Streets. The voice on the other end of the telephone said, "Don't give away my part in the Christmas pageant this year. I plan to be a wise man one last time."

So began the journey of an 81-year-old man who had been one of the wise men in our live Christmas Eve nativity tableau over the years. It was to be his last journey to the manger—a journey that was just as difficult as the long one across the desert made by the magi so many years ago. You see, Mr. Laws was dying of cancer.

He had been poor most of his life, living alone at Third and Race Streets in a shack behind a leather goods store. His house had neither indoor plumbing nor central heating. The place was so ramshackle that it was not advisable for him to return there in his poor state of health. But his Medicare coverage at the hospital was running out, and he had to move. Would we take him in at Old First?

At that time the church parsonage was vacant. With the Board's permission, the church agreed to have a hospital bed, commode, and other simple furniture installed in the living room to accommodate our longtime neighbor. The hospital promised home nursing care on a regular basis.

Mr. Laws had made the Old City neighborhood his home since the early 1920s. Sometimes his wife joined him on her days off. She was a live-in maid in a rich suburb. After some years he was estranged from her, from his children, and from most of his relatives. He became a real loner. But when he needed help, he always came to the church.

In fact, he had come to see me in May, complaining of a problem in his throat. I took him to the hospital, but when the doctors wanted to do more tests, he refused and checked himself out. It wasn't until he got an infection in his legs and couldn't walk that he sent someone around to the church with word that Mr. Laws needed help. When I arrived at his house and saw him sitting on his step, unable to stand, I called an ambulance. After some days at the hospital his legs began to clear up, but it was then that the doctors discovered the real problem—a malignant tumor in his esophagus.

In many ways Mr. Laws was an original street person. He loved to sit on the step to the walkway leading to his house and watch the comings and goings of everyone who lived within the twenty square blocks of "his" corner. He could recount stories of happenings on the main streets, as well as in the alleys of Old City, going back more than sixty years. In the hospital he used to love to keep me at his bedside past the time I had planned to stay, with "just one more story."

But now Mr. Laws was confined to his bed in the parsonage most of the time. He spent several hours each day hooked up to a machine that pumped the daily amount of liquid nutrient needed to keep him alive. He could no longer roam about freely. Instead he had to wait for friends to visit him. Oftentimes he was disappointed that more people didn't take the time to stop and chat. He could hear them rush past his door, and he was left alone inside with no one to listen to his many memories of years gone by.

I was able to bring a few precious possessions from his old house to the parsonage. He asked me to put some of his favorite pictures on a piece of posterboard, which I set on the mantel. He wanted his portable TV set moved in, and although I wasn't fond of the idea, he insisted on keeping his shotgun next to his bed. This man knew urban life and wanted to be ready to handle any situation.

One of the mementos Mr. Laws was proudest of was a photo taken at our outdoor Christmas creche. It was the one year we had had a live camel. Mr. Laws had arranged for his picture to be snapped as he kissed the camel. He thought it was very clever for a wise man to be caught kissing his camel!

The idea of being a wise man really shaped Mr. Laws over the years. At first he took the role rather lightly. The pastor of Old First had to go out and search diligently for him on many a Christmas Eve. On those occasions the pastor had to pour several cups of hot coffee into Mr. Laws so that he would be able to walk the one block from his home to the church for the Christmas Eve tableau. But over the years the role stuck, and Mr. Laws identified with the magi, astrologers who watched the sky, rather than the street, for signs of profound happenings in their world.

The last year of his life Mr. Laws made the trip to the manger with all the intensity of the original wise men. At this point it was not easy for him to walk. He had had radiation treatments for several months, and they had weakened him considerably. The weather was very, very cold that particular Christmas Eve. It had reached several degrees below zero. Even younger, healthier people were reluctant to come out. Mr. Laws dressed for the cold weather, layering several sets of clothing and putting on heavy rubber boots over his shoes. He was the second person to arrive at the Parish House; one of the shepherds was already there, putting on his shepherd costume.

Mr. Laws found the familiar robes of the magi and struggled into one, with the help of his nurse, who had come along for moral support. It wasn't easy to fit the robe over the layers of clothing he already was wearing. When he was dressed, we placed a turban on his head, and he was ready. He patiently waited for the other wise men to arrive.

Mary and Joseph entered the creche with the baby, right on cue. Next came the shepherds, hoping that a few sheep would respond and follow with them. Then came the wise men, all three, with Mr. Laws bringing up the rear. He walked carefully, stumbling slightly with each step. He carried an urn filled with myrrh, a bitter-tasting substance used to anoint the dead in Jesus' day. When Mr. Laws came to the place where the baby lay, he bowed and, with all the dignity he could muster, fell down on his knees as he faced the new life in the creche. No longer was he playing the part. This time it was for real. He had seen the light of life and had followed it once again to the Christmas creche. Noticing its young beauty, he responded with awe. Pondering its tremendous potential, he knelt in humility. Attracted by the love embodied there, he paused to worship.

Mr. Laws made the final journey into the presence of God just six weeks later. He had, however, already caught a glimpse of God's glory as, year after year, he made the journey to the manger as a wise man.

15

The Fourth Wise Man

JANE, ONE OF OUR senior members, who has passed the ninety-year mark and is still going strong, likes to recite Henry Van Dyke's classic Christmas tale, *The Story of the Other Wise Man*. She has memorized most of it and enjoys reciting it when I visit her.

In the story Van Dyke postulates a fourth wise man, who sets out to meet the other magi in search of the newborn king. This wise man, however, never makes it to the Bethlehem stable with the other three. Instead, he stops along the way to help people. He finally arrives in Jerusalem thirty-three years later, on a somber Passover Friday, and learns that the king is on a Calvary hill, nailed to a cross to die.

Old First has a fourth wise man too. Bob has a great sense of drama and also a sense of humor. He is one of our church's active deacons, heading the social concerns committee and specifically being involved in the homeless program. His travels take him to other churches, where he describes the needs of "the least of these" and encourages participation in feeding, clothing, and sheltering the men in whom he has seen the Christ.

Every Christmas, Bob crosses the Benjamin Franklin Bridge from Camden, New Jersey to Philadelphia to make his pilgrimage to the manger. He dresses the part, putting on full, flowing robes to indicate his kingly stature. After parking his car some distance from the church, he comes on foot, bearing his gifts for the newborn child. Customers in nearby restaurants, comfortably sipping cups of coffee at sunny windows, stand up and crane their necks to see the sight. Bystanders move out of the way. Who's this coming down Fourth Street? One expects to see Santa Claus roaming the city streets at Christmastime, but who's this character?

Dramatically, Bob enters the creche, bows before the manger, and humbly leaves his gifts. Then he takes his position among the mannequins as the fourth wise man in the scene. Hours on end he stands there immobile, occasionally relaxing his pose long enough to greet the startled crowd gathered around the creche. And then he disappears. The rest of the year he continues his work, seeking to minister to the least and the lonely through our social concerns committee.

A memorable moment at the Christmas creche was a visit of a whole group of mentally retarded young adults. Bob couldn't see them at first, but he felt their presence to his right. When he left his place with the mannequins, he found the group lining the fence. "Each person had to touch me, all down the line," Bob reported. "It was a moving experience on both sides of the fence as a strong bond developed between us."

16

A Meeting Place for Unity

FATHER WATTERS, pastor of Old St. Joseph's Church, just four blocks south of Old First at Fourth and Walnut Streets, asked me to visit his Roman Catholic congregation in celebration of the Week of Prayer for Christian Unity. The year before, he and some of his parishioners had attended our regular Sunday morning worship at Old First in observance of the same event. Now he wanted me and some of our Old First members to reciprocate. He suggested that I address his congregation after their traditional parochial mass on the Sunday marking the end of the Unity Octave.

As we were conversing in preparation for my visit, Father Watters shared his interest in Pope John Paul II's five-day meeting with Orthodox Patriarch of Constantinople Demetrios I in Istanbul. This was the first time that the leaders of these two communions had met for face-to-face dialogue in which issues of substance were discussed, Father Watters reported. The ecumenical movement for the Roman Church is two-directional—toward the Protestants and toward the Orthodox.

My mind flashed back to our Christmas creche. The Sunday before Christmas, after our service of worship, I was still in the church building when two persons appeared at our front door. One man had walked up the street after mass at Old St. Joseph's Church. The other man, from St. Michael the Archangel Russian Orthodox Church, four blocks north at Fourth Street and Fairmount Avenue, was returning to his New Jersey home after the divine liturgy and decided to stop to see our creche close up. Both men met at the manger and together came inside to visit our sanctuary. A few Old

First members were present as well, and spontaneously a lively, ecumenical conversation ensued.

Perhaps our ecumenical dialogue will proceed more smoothly if we are able to meet informally at the creche. We need to remember that it is Christ's *life* we share—his birth, death, and resurrection—and *not* a set of dogmas. So often our ecumenical conversation disintegrates into a deadly discussion because we concentrate on working through the doctrinal differences that divide us. We so easily forget that it is Christ's life that animates our faith. If we put Christ's life at the center of our dialogue, Christ will give us the momentum we need to work for real, visible unity in the church.

17

Go, Tell It!

IN FRANCE THERE IS a tradition of making *santons,* little wooden or ceramic figurines that depict all the people of the Christmas story. Of course, there are the shepherds, wise men, Mary, Joseph, and the infant Jesus, just as we have in our own creche. But the French also include figurines that represent all the people of the town. There are garbage collectors, teachers, cooks, police, street vendors, nurses, clerks, factory workers—all the people who live in the town are there, dressed in contemporary clothing. The French are saying that we are all there—you and I are part of the story!

This is also true of our live creche at Fourth and Race Streets. So many people gather there. The circle around the manger is very wide and includes all who come, all the people of our city. No one is an outsider at the creche. All of us who stand there are in the story too. The story pulls us in, begs our participation, touches our lives. Maybe that is why so many people want to feed the animals. They want to be connected, to be involved with the scene, in some way.

Once the story has touched us, it is easy to go tell it—to go and share it with others. We cannot keep to ourselves for long what we have seen and felt; instinctively we want to spread the news.

Children illustrate this best. They immediately want to talk about what they have seen or heard or done. Maybe that is why they cannot keep secrets. They have to spread the news to all. They are the best broadcasters and evangelists.

The news media also know a good story when they see one. That is their business. None of the TV stations in Philadelphia misses the chance to come to Fourth and Race to film our nativity scene. The very first weekend the animals arrive the story is on the air. The reporters interview people who come to see. Little five-year-old Hannah was there one Saturday morning with her sister and her dad. The public television cameras came, and she got to tell the Christmas story over the air several times during the holiday season.

I am always impressed by the beautiful and profound thoughts that TV personalities and newspaper columnists use to describe our creche. Some of them know little about the details of the original story. But something has moved and touched them—and *they* are the ones who automatically invite others to come and see for themselves.

Ultimately the event of Christ's birth, God's coming in human form, is not something we can hold onto for ourselves. It is not a private story. Christ came for the whole world, and Christ's birth opens us up to go ahead and tell it, to spread the word!

Publicity for our live creche is not something we have to be concerned about. It just happens by word of mouth or through the media—the news is out. Christ is born!

18

Lessons in Caring

SHEEP ARE STRANGE ANIMALS. Every Christmas I have a chance to observe them close up as I come and go, hurrying past the creche at different hours of the day and night, or as I gaze at them from a distance through my office window.

One year, each of the three sheep arrived wearing an earring. I don't know what the earrings signified, but I laughed when I first saw them. These sheep will fit very well into urban life, I thought. They look so sophisticated, with an earring dangling from one ear.

Sheep are so different from the other animals in the stable. The cow is always out front, stealing the show. You *have* to notice her. The donkeys are so cute. Their playful nature gets them a lot of attention. But where are the sheep? They are such shy animals. They're usually hiding in the back of the creche. They don't come out readily. You have to practically scare them or chase them to get them moving, and then they all run out at once. Where one goes, they all go.

I have the habit of watching other sheep as well. These are the ones about whom the psalmist wrote, "We are God's people; the sheep of God's pasture." These are the ones who have been entrusted to me. I'm constantly looking after them. And as I look, I see that some of them are beginning to change their ways. They are beginning to take care of one another. They are learning the lessons of caring through their involvement in the Christmas creche.

Of course, there are the obvious shepherds. Janet and Connie stop each morning on their way to work to feed the animals. It's a job that has to be done *every* morning, seven days a week. There's no chance to sleep in. So on Saturdays and Sundays, too, they come to fill the water pans and put out the corn mixture. At times they have to climb the fence and go into the stable to fix the mannequins—to put Mary back together again when she falls apart or to stand Joseph upright when he leans too far in one direction. Jackie has the evening shift, arriving from the office with briefcase in hand. She rakes the straw out of the water troughs, replenishes the water, and fills the manger with hay.

There's also the crew that builds the creche. Earl and John provide the leadership, but they're learning to recruit younger men too. The pieces of the creche are heavy, requiring muscle power. Barry, John's son-in-law, has gotten involved and has brought friends who aren't even related to Old First.

The night of the pageant a whole host of people come out. There are those "good sports" who don the special robes to play the parts of shepherds, wise men, and holy family. Even 87-year-old Owen got involved once. Marion brings an assortment of bells to provide appropriate sound effects. Ruth helps to keep everything running on schedule, and Connie and Janet return to prevent an unruly cow from getting out of hand.

Over the weekends, Saturdays and Sundays before Christmas, many Old First members come to the manger to serve as welcomers for the hundreds of visitors. Our members hand out fliers and invite people to return on Christmas Eve for the outdoor live tableau and the traditional carol service in the church. They offer cups of hot chocolate and a chance to chat in the Parish House. They tell about our church and take people inside for a look at the sanctuary. It's not just one or two persons who are there to greet visitors; whole families take on the job. Actually the children lead the way because they are naturally open and enthusiastic. Members of all ages, Phyllis, Jennifer, Dick, John and Judy and family, Bob and his daughters, enjoy this special way to be involved with the Christmas story. Sally managed to squeeze more than twenty persons into the small outer office of the Parish House and to serve them hot chocolate one Saturday morning. It looked like they were having a party. Everyone was speaking at once—in Chinese! Another day I asked Miae, "How did it go?" I knew she was learning about pastoring when she laughed, "Geneva, there were so many people that finally we had to lock the door and leave." Yes, that's how it is when you begin to get involved with tending sheep.

Last year something new was added, a Children's Christmas Workshop—three hours of crafts, puppets, songs, stories, explaining the message behind the creche and the meaning of Christ's birth to children and their parents. One unchurched family exclaimed, "Gee, this was great! We could have bought $40 tickets to a Christmas show and not had as much fun." The whole project was planned and carried out by church people who don't normally work with children.

As I observed all this activity going on around the creche, I was struck by the basic joy and enthusiasm everybody brought to the tasks. No one said, "I can't do this," or "That is too difficult for me." Everyone was creative in finding a way to do the job in her or his own unique style. Everybody wanted to be involved in some way. No one said, "I don't have time," or asked, "What's this all about?" Members discovered the meaning as they went along. No one felt more important than another but recognized how we all are part of this project, which is obviously so much bigger than any one of us.

The best part was that Old First members forgot about themselves and reached out to relate to those who were coming, sensing and serving their needs. They welcomed the stranger with interest and eagerness. Relating to people is at the heart of ministry. It's not the committees we serve on, although they're important. It's not the basic work we do, although that's necessary. It's how we relate to one another in doing the work or serving on the committees that is what pastoring is all about. Our jobs are not to be bosses, ordering one another around, but partners as we relate to others in all the things we do as the church.

Now, if we can do all this so naturally and so enthusiastically two weeks out of the year, wouldn't it be wonderful if we could do it all year long? Why not show the same joy and eagerness and willingness and sensitivity and commitment to our work as the church throughout the year?

Jesus says, "Love your neighbor."

Paul admonishes us to "bear one another's burdens."

Because we are willing to work together, we *become* the living creche. We become God's love incarnate. We embody the incarnation as God continues to love the world through us, the living body of Christ.

I've often remarked that the living Christmas creche is Old First's gift to all the people of Philadelphia at Christmastime. But now I've begun to discover that the Christmas creche is also God's gift to us. Through the creche and the activities around it, all of us are learning the lessons of caring and are discovering how to work together to be the living, loving church of Jesus Christ.

A Tradition Continues

THE FENCE AROUND THE CRECHE includes plaques with readings from the prophet Isaiah announcing the promised Messiah, and from the Christmas narrative in Luke's Gospel announcing Jesus' birth. But the words of the noted black preacher Howard Thurman, also printed on one of the plaques, bring the Christmas message to our contemporary world with startling clarity. Thurman writes about the meaning of Christmas:

> *It is the brooding Presence of the Eternal Spirit*
> *making crooked paths straight, rough places smooth,*
> *tired hearts refreshed, dead hopes stirred with the*
> *newness of life. It is the promise of tomorrow at*
> *the close of every day, the movement of life in defiance*
> *of death, and the assurance that love is sturdier*
> *than hate, that right is more confident than wrong,*
> *that good is more permanent than evil. . . .*
>
> *I will light the candle of fellowship this Christmas.*
> *I know that the experiences of unity in human relations*
> *are more compelling than the concepts, the fears,*
> *the prejudices, which divide. Despite the tendency to*
> *feel my race superior, my nation the greatest nation,*
> *my faith the true faith, I must beat down the*
> *boundaries of my exclusiveness until my sense of*
> *separateness is completely enveloped in a sense of*
> *fellowship. There must be free and easy access by all,*

---

to all the rich resources accumulated by groups and
individuals in years of living and experiencing.
I will light the candle of fellowship this Christmas,
a candle that must burn all the year long.